TEAM SPIRIT

SMART BOOKS FOR YOUNG FANS

T0244916

THE NEW YORK KNICKS

BY
MARK STEWART

NORWOODHOUSE PRESS

Norwood House Press
2544 Clinton Street
Buffalo, NY 14224

Photos courtesy of: Getty Images (Cover, 4, 14, 25, 35 bottom), Associated Press (6, 8, 9, 10, 12, 24, 27, 31, 35 top left, 36, 37, 41, 42, 43 both, 45), Upper Case Editorial (7, 18, 22, 38), Author's Collection (11, 19, 21, 28, 34 left, 35 top right), Topps, Inc. (15, 17, 34 right), Capitol Cards (26, 39), New York Knicks (29), Bowman Gum Co. (30), SLAM Magazine (33).

The memorabilia, artifacts, and media images that are pictured in this book are presented for educational and informational purposes and come from the collection of the author.

Art Director: Lisa Miley
Series Design: Ron Jaffe
Project Management: Upper Case Editorial Services LLC
Special thanks to Topps, Inc.

Names: Stewart, Mark, 1960 July 7-.
Title: The New York Knicks / Mark Stewart.
Description: Buffalo, NY : Norwood House Press, 2025. | Series: Team spirit | Includes glossary and index.
Identifiers: ISBN 978-1-6845-0093-2 (pbk.) | ISBN 978-1-6845-0094-9 (library bound) | ISBN 978-1-6845-0095-6 (ebook)
Subjects: LCSH: New York Knickerbockers (Basketball team)--Juvenile literature. | New York Knickerbockers (Basketball team)--History--Juvenile literature.
Classification: LCC GV885.52.N4 S84 2025 | DDC 796.323'64--dc23

378N—022324
Manufactured in the United States of America in North Mankato, Minnesota.

TABLE OF CONTENTS

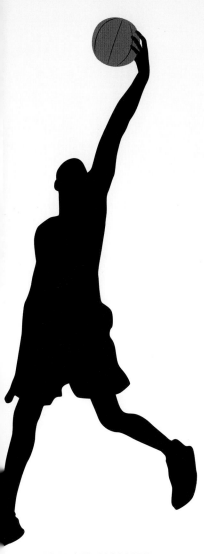

ABOUT OUR GLOSSARY

In this book, there may be several words that you are reading for the first time. Some are sports words, some are new vocabulary words, and some are familiar words that are used in an unusual way. All of these words are defined on page 46. Throughout the book, sports words appear in **bold type**. Regular vocabulary words appear in *bold italic type*.

NYC
NEW YORK
5
22
NYC
sphere
NEW YORK
11
NYC
sphere
NEW YORK
3
NYC
KNICKS

MAKING THE KNICKS

Basketball is a team game based on individual skills. Not everyone can be a superstar, but a superstar cannot win on his own either. That is why team *chemistry* is so important. The New York Knicks are at their best when they share the ball and let each athlete do what he does best.

To make the Knicks, a player must have the ability to take charge when the time is right, but also the willingness to play *unselfish* basketball. When the team finds the right mix, they are hard to stop and a lot of fun to watch.

This book tells the story of the Knicks. They expect their leaders to make amazing plays on the court. They also count on them to keep their teammates focused and energized. After all, in a city where millions of fans "eat, drink, and sleep" basketball, representing the orange and blue is a job the Knicks do 24 hours a day.

Precious Achiuwa and Josh Hart exchange a look of disbelief after a great play by Jalen Brunson. The Knicks are at their best when they have strong team leaders like Brunson.

BUILDING BLOCKS

When the **Basketball Association of America (BAA)** formed in 1946, people everywhere kept a close eye on the New York Knickerbockers, or "Knicks" for short. To be successful, the new league needed a strong team in New York. The Knicks turned out to be one of the best teams in the BAA. They continued their fine play after the BAA joined forces with the older **National Basketball League (NBL)** to form the **National Basketball Association (NBA)**.

Much of the credit for New York's success went to the team's coach, Joe Lapchick. He had been a legendary player in the 1920s and a very popular college coach after that. Lapchick demanded that the Knicks play as a team. As a result, New York made it to the **playoffs** in each of Lapchick's eight seasons. They reached the **NBA Finals** three times in a row, from 1950–51 to 1952–53.

The stars of those early clubs included Harry Gallatin, Dick

McGuire, Carl Braun, Vince Boryla, Max Zaslofsky, Ray Felix, Connie Simmons, Ernie Vandeweghe, and Nat "Sweetwater" Clifton. These were some of the biggest names in basketball at the time. Clifton was the first African American star in the NBA.

In the years that followed, many more good players wore the New York uniform, including Richie Guerin, Kenny Sears, Willie Naulls, and Johnny Green. However, the Knicks fell behind other NBA teams during the late 1950s and early 1960s. At one point, they suffered eight losing seasons in a row. Finally, New York began to rebuild around a group of talented and unselfish college stars, including Willis Reed, Bill Bradley, Cazzie Russell, Walt Frazier, Phil Jackson, and Dave Stallworth. Trades for Dave DeBusschere, Dick Barnett, Jerry Lucas, and Earl Monroe made the Knicks even better. Under coach Red Holzman, they became NBA champions in 1970 and again in 1973.

As these stars retired, the Knicks found other exciting players, including Bob McAdoo, Spencer Haywood, Ray Williams, Micheal

LEFT: Dick McGuire played point guard for the Knicks in the 1950s.
ABOVE: Dave DeBusschere battles for a loose ball.

Ray Richardson, Bill Cartwright, and Bernard King. The Knicks played winning basketball, but they were never a serious championship **contender**. The team did not return to the NBA Finals until the 1990s.

By then, New York had a new coach and a new star. Pat Riley, who had guided the Los Angeles Lakers to four championships during the 1980s, was hired to coach the team. Patrick Ewing, a fierce center, led a tough, defensive-minded club that included Mark Jackson, Charles Oakley, Anthony Mason, and John Starks. Ewing and the Knicks had a *bitter* rivalry with Michael Jordan and the Chicago Bulls. Unfortunately, New York usually came out on the short end of the score when they played. However, the Knicks reached the NBA Finals in 1994, and came within a basket of beating the Houston Rockets for the championship.

The Knicks returned to the NBA Finals in the spring of 1999. Ewing was still the team leader. His teammates now included **All-Stars** Larry Johnson, Allan Houston, and Latrell Sprewell. Once again, New York fell short of the championship, this time losing to

LEFT: Most fans agree that Patrick Ewing was the best player in team history.
ABOVE: Bernard King drives to the basket.

the San Antonio Spurs in five games. Ewing played his final season in New York in 1999–2000. He retired as the team's all-time leader in scoring and rebounding.

The Knicks began the 2000s looking to put together another winning group. Finding players who wanted to call New York "home" was not a problem. There is nothing quite like playing in Madison Square Garden when all the seats are filled. New York fans know their basketball. When a player does well, he is *showered* with love. But when things are not going the team's way, those same fans are not shy about sharing their disappointment. Many of the players that joined the Knicks did not do well under this pressure. Year after year, the team struggled to find the right mix.

From 2001–02 to 2009–10, the Knicks did not have a single winning season. Their stars during this time included Nate Robinson, David Lee, and Stephon Marbury. Marbury was born in nearby Brooklyn. He was a great **ball-handler** and scorer. Beginning in 2010–11, the Knicks returned to the playoffs three years in a row. The difference-makers were Amar'e Stoudemire and Carmelo Anthony. The two superstars came to the Knicks in big trades.

Like Marbury, Anthony learned the game in Brooklyn. Anthony was an All-Star every year he played for the Knicks. Stoudemire and Anthony were joined by *rugged* center Tyson Chandler, who was named NBA Defensive Player of the Year. In 2012–13, Anthony led the league in scoring and the Knicks won 54 games. They finished atop the **Atlantic Division** for the first time since the 1990s.

Injuries, poor trades, and bad luck struck the Knicks in the years that followed. Things finally changed for the better in 2020–21, when the team made Tom Thibodeau its coach. Thibodeau molded young stars Julius Randle, Mitchell Robinson, Jalen Brunson, and RJ Barrett into a winning team with a bright future. As the Knicks add new players and continue to improve, New York fans should have much to cheer about in the years to come.

LEFT: Allan Houston and Latrell Sprewell starred for the Knicks when they reached the 1999 NBA Finals. **ABOVE**: Amar'e Stoudemire, Carmelo Anthony, and Tyson Chandler signed this photo.

GAME DAY

The Knicks have called Madison Square Garden home since their first season. But they have played in two buildings with that name. The team's current "MSG" opened during the 1967–68 season. It is considered America's most famous basketball arena.

In the first Madison Square Garden, the Knicks sometimes took a backseat to more popular events, including hockey games and the circus. When two events were scheduled at once, the Knicks had to find another place to play. Often, they used a local *armory*.

BY THE NUMBERS

- The Knicks' arena has 19,812 seats for basketball.

- As of 2023–24, the Knicks had retired seven uniform numbers: 10 (Walt Frazier), 12 (Dick Barnett), 15 (Earl Monroe & Dick McGuire), 19 (Willis Reed), 22 (Dave DeBusschere), 24 (Bill Bradley), and 33 (Patrick Ewing). No player can wear those numbers again. The team also retired 613—the number of games won by coach Red Holzman.

- The Knicks' arena was modernized in 2014 at a cost of $297 million.

The Knicks battle the Miami Heat at Madison Square Garden.

TEAM COLORS

The Knicks wear uniforms that feature orange and blue. Those are also the *official* colors of New York City. For many years, NBA teams wore light-colored home uniforms. The Knicks wore white tops and bottoms with orange and blue letters and numbers. In recent years, NBA teams have switched to dark colors at home. The Knicks typically wear blue when they play at Madison Square Garden.

WILLIE NAULLS   NEW YORK Knicks

The team got its name from the club's founder, Ned Irish. For almost 20 years, the team's official *logo* showed a *colonial* New Yorker (or Knickerbocker) dribbling a basketball. The name was shortened to "Knicks" so it could fit on a uniform. In 1964, the Knickerbocker logo was replaced. New York's logo has gone through several changes since then.

LEFT: Mitchell Robinson wears the 2024 road uniform. For many years, the Knicks wore white at home. **ABOVE**: Willie Naulls wears the team's blue road uniform from the late 1950s.

LAST TEAM STANDING

At the end of a basketball season, there can only be one team left standing. That team is the winner of the NBA Finals. In their early years, the Knicks came very close, but could not win the championship series. They made it to the NBA Finals three times in the early 1950s but lost each time. They were defeated by the Rochester Royals (now Sacramento Kings) once and the Minneapolis Lakers (who now play in Los Angeles) twice.

In 1968–69, many New York fans believed their young, exciting team would return to the NBA Finals. Unfortunately, they lost to the more experienced Boston Celtics, who went on to win the championship. Coach Red Holzman made sure his team was ready to play in 1969–70. New York's leaders were center Willis Reed, forward Dave DeBusschere, and guard Walt Frazier. They were joined by forwards Bill Bradley, Dave Stallworth, and Cazzie Russell, and guards Dick Barnett and Mike Riordan.

Each of these players was good enough to be a star on another team. Their coach taught them how to be part of something much greater. Holzman *urged* his players to keep passing the ball until they found an open man. Because everyone on the team could shoot well, the Knicks were very hard to defend. Holzman also taught his team a complicated defense. Often, right in the middle of the action, two New York teammates would "switch" the players they were guarding. This confused the opponent and put less strain on the defense.

The Knicks won 60 games during the 1969–70 season—more than any other team in the NBA. They beat the Baltimore Bullets (now the Washington Wizards) in a tough first-round playoff series. Next, New York faced the Milwaukee Bucks and their 7' 2" center, Kareem Abdul-Jabbar. Reed battled Abdul-Jabbar one-on-one, while the rest of the Knicks outplayed the Bucks. New York won the series easily.

The Knicks met the Lakers in the NBA Finals. Reed faced another great center in Wilt Chamberlain, and again he held his own. With series tied after four games, Reed injured his leg in

ABOVE: This trading card shows the Knicks celebrating their first NBA title.

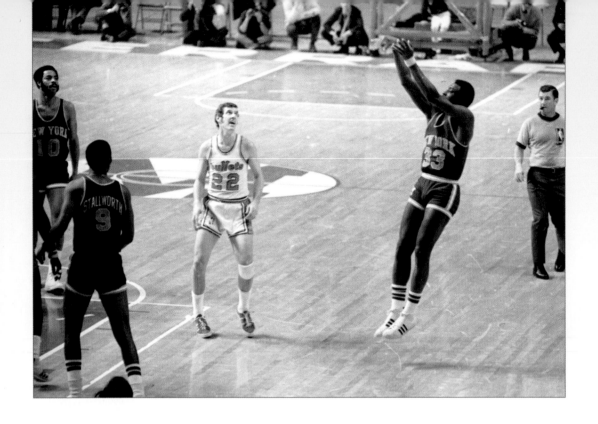

Game 5. Chamberlain took advantage and the Lakers forced the series to a winner-take-all Game 7. It looked like all was lost for New York, but to everyone's surprise, Reed limped onto the court. The Lakers could not believe their eyes. Reed's *presence* provided the spark in a 113–99 victory. All of New York celebrated the Knicks' first NBA championship.

The Knicks and Lakers faced each other again in the 1972 NBA Finals. This time Los Angeles won. At the end of the 1972–73 season, the two teams met for the championship for a third time in four seasons. The Knicks had added future Hall of Famers Earl Monroe and Jerry Lucas. Like the other Knicks, Monroe and Lucas accepted smaller roles that gave New York the best chance to win. The Knicks' strategy was to wear Chamberlain down. Reed did an excellent job making him work hard for every shot and every rebound. Meanwhile, the rest of the team played brilliant defense. The Lakers won the opening game but the Knicks **swept** the next four to win their second championship, 4 games to 1.

The Knicks reached the NBA Finals again in 1994. They were led by another great center, Patrick Ewing. New York faced the Houston Rockets in a thrilling series that went seven games. Unfortunately, the Knicks lost the championship in a close game on Houston's home court. Five years later, the Knicks returned to the NBA Finals. This time, they were defeated by the San Antonio Spurs.

LEFT: Walt Frazier and Dave Stallworth watch as Cazzie Russell releases a jump shot. Teamwork was the key to New York's success.
ABOVE: Earl Monroe battles Jerry West of the Lakers on the cover of the team's 1973 yearbook.

LEADING LIGHTS

Some players lead with their words. Others lead with their actions. The greatest Knicks inspired their teammates and thrilled New York fans by doing both. They are the team's brightest stars.

CARL BRAUN   6´ 5″ Guard

• BORN: 9/25/1927   • DIED: 2/10/2010   • PLAYED FOR TEAM: 1947–48 TO 1960–61

Carl Braun was one of the tallest guards of the 1950s. He missed two seasons while serving in the military, but was an All-Star four years in a row when he returned. Braun was the team's top scorer seven times.

DICK McGUIRE   6´ 6″ Guard

• BORN: 1/25/1926   • DIED: 2/3/2010   • PLAYED FOR TEAM: 1949–50 TO 1956–57

Dick McGuire was nicknamed "Tricky Dick" for his lightning-fast dribbling and quick passes. He led the Knicks to the NBA Finals three seasons in a row. McGuire entered the Hall of Fame in 1993.

RICHIE GUERIN   6´ 4˝ Guard

- Born 5/29/1932
- Played for Team: 1956–57 to 1963–64

Richie Guerin played guard but scored and rebounded like a forward. He was almost impossible to defend. Guerin averaged more than 20 points a game four seasons in a row, including a 29.5 scoring average in 1961–62.

WILLIS REED   6´ 10˝ Center

- Born: 6/25/1942 • Died: 3/21/2023
- Played for Team: 1964–65 to 1973–74

Willis Reed was a great all-around star. Few centers were as *versatile*. His shooting, rebounding, defense, and leadership helped the Knicks win two NBA championships.

WALT FRAZIER   6´ 4˝ Guard

- Born: 3/29/1945 • Played for Team: 1967–68 to 1976–77

Walt Frazier had style on and off the court. He was a big, strong guard who was also very quick. Frazier was an excellent shooter and ball-handler, and one of the best defensive players in the NBA.

ABOVE: Richie Guerin signed this photo from the early 1960s.

BILL BRADLEY   6´ 5˝ Forward

- BORN: 7/28/1943   • PLAYED FOR TEAM: 1967–68 TO 1976–77

Had Bill Bradley played for another team, he might have finished among the NBA scoring leaders most years. With the Knicks, he used his skills to make his teammates better. That earned Bradley a place in the Basketball Hall of Fame.

DAVE DeBUSSCHERE   6´ 6˝ Forward

- BORN: 10/16/1940   • DIED: 5/14/2003
- PLAYED FOR TEAM: 1968–69 TO 1973–74

Dave DeBusschere was the final *ingredient* in New York's rise to the NBA championship. He was a skilled defender and rebounder, and had an excellent jump shot. In DeBusschere's first full season with the Knicks, they won their first championship.

EARL MONROE   6´ 3˝ Guard

- BORN: 11/21/1944
- PLAYED FOR TEAM: 1971–72 TO 1979–80

Earl Monroe was nicknamed "The Pearl." He was the NBA's flashiest player before he joined the Knicks. Monroe changed his style to fit in with the Knicks and helped them win the NBA championship in 1973.

Earl Monroe flicks the ball toward the rim.

BERNARD KING   6´ 7˝ Forward

• Born: 12/4/1956   • Played for Team: 1982–83 to 1986–87

Bernard King was one of the NBA's truly "unstoppable" scorers. He **released** his shot so quickly that defenders had no chance to block it. In 1984–85, he scored 60 points in a game and became the first Knick to lead the NBA in scoring.

PATRICK EWING   7´ 0˝ Center

• Born: 8/5/1962   • Played for Team: 1985–86 to 1999–2000

Patrick Ewing was a *dominant* defender in college. When he joined the Knicks, he proved he was an equally talented scorer. Ewing's leadership helped the Knicks reach the NBA Finals twice. He was an All-Star 12 times.

CHARLES OAKLEY   6´ 8˝ Forward

• Born: 12/18/1963   • Played for Team: 1988–89 to 1997–98

Charles Oakley was one of the hardest-working players in the NBA. When a ball was loose anywhere near "Oak," chances were good that it would end up in his hands. Oakley was an excellent rebounder and one of the NBA's best defensive players.

JOHN STARKS   6´ 3˝ Guard

• Born: 8/10/1965   • Played for Team: 1990–91 to 1997–98

John Starks played for four different colleges and three *professional* teams before he came to the Knicks. He finally found his basketball home in New York. Starks played with great heart and became a fan favorite in Madison Square Garden.

ALLAN HOUSTON
6′ 6″ Guard

• BORN: 4/20/1971 • PLAYED FOR TEAM: 1996–97 TO 2004–05

Allan Houston was a deadly *accurate* shooter. As the son of a college basketball coach, he had a great understanding of the game. Houston teamed up with Latrell Sprewell to give the Knicks a good one-two scoring punch.

CARMELO ANTHONY
6′ 8″ Forward

• BORN: 5/29/1984 • PLAYED FOR TEAM: 2010–11 TO 2016–17

Carmelo Anthony was an All-Star in each of his seven seasons with the Knicks. In 2012–13, he averaged 28.7 points per game to win the NBA scoring championship. Although the team struggled to win, "Melo" enjoyed his time in New York, where he was born and raised.

AMAR'E STOUDEMIRE
6′ 10″ Forward

• BORN: 11/16/1982

• PLAYED FOR TEAM: 2010–11 TO 2014–15

In the summer of 2010, the Knicks went shopping for a superstar. They traded for Amar'e Stoudemire and, in his first year in New York, he set a team record by scoring 30 or more points nine games in a row. Knee problems slowed Stoudemire down for much of his time with the club, but when he was healthy, he was one of the best scorers in the NBA.

ABOVE: Amar'e Stoudemire offers advice to teammate Iman Shumpert.
RIGHT: Julius Randle and Jalen Brunson attack the defense during a 2024 game.

RJ BARRETT
6′ 6″ Guard

- BORN: 6/14/2000 • PLAYED FOR TEAM: 2019–20 TO 2023–24

After being named Player of the Year in his first college season, RJ Barrett decided to enter the NBA at age 19. He showed he was ready for the pros and improved quickly. In 2021–22, Barrett became the youngest Knick to average more than 20 points a game.

JULIUS RANDLE
6′ 8″ Forward

- BORN: 11/29/1994
- FIRST SEASON WITH TEAM: 2019–20

When the Knicks signed Julius Randle, many New York fans had never heard of him. That soon changed when he was picked for the All-Star Game and was named the NBA's Most Improved Player in 2020. Randle only got better, often scoring between 20 and 30 points a game.

JALEN BRUNSON
6′ 2″ Guard

- BORN: 8/31/1996
- FIRST SEASON WITH TEAM: 2022–23

Jalen Brunson helped his college team win two national championships. The Knicks believed he could be their next great leader. In Brunson's first two seasons in New York, he averaged over 20 points a game and led the team in assists. In 2024, he was named an NBA All-Star for the first time.

X'S AND O'S

The goal of every NBA coach is to get his team to the NBA Finals. Four coaches have led the Knicks to the championship round. The first was Joe Lapchick. Long before there was an NBA, he starred for a team called the New York Celtics. They traveled all

over the country to help *promote* the sport of basketball. With Lapchick calling the shots, the Knicks reached the NBA Finals each year from 1951 to 1953.

Red Holzman led the Knicks to the NBA Finals three times in the 1970s, and the team won the championship twice. Holzman found ways to mix old-time *strategies* with modern playing styles. In an *era* when most players focused on scoring, he convinced the Knicks to pass the ball on offense and work together on defense. Holzman won more than 600 games in New York.

In 1994, the Knicks went to the NBA Finals under Pat Riley. Riley had coached the Los Angeles Lakers in the 1980s when the team was known for its fast-paced "Showtime" style. In New York, he asked his players to slow the game down. The Knicks relied on strength and toughness to wear down opponents and win games.

Jeff Van Gundy took over for Riley in 1995. Four years later, he guided the Knicks to the NBA Finals. Van Gundy was a shy, quiet man, but he taught his players to be extra-*aggressive* at all times. Under Van Gundy, the Knicks were one of the league's most difficult teams to play.

One of Van Gundy's assistants was Tom Thibodeau. Thibodeau went on to coach the Chicago Bulls and was named NBA Coach of the Year in 2010–11. In 2020, "Thibs" returned to New York as head coach of the Knicks. The team went from 21 wins to 41 in one season and Thibodeau was named Coach of the Year again!

LEFT: Joe Lapchick led the Knicks to the NBA Finals three times.
ABOVE: Pat Riley coached the Knicks in the early 1990s.

When the 1969–70 NBA playoffs began, Willis Reed knew he had a rough job ahead of him. The Knicks' 6' 10" center would have to face a pair of Hall of Famers just to reach the NBA Finals: Wes Unseld of the Baltimore Bullets and Kareem Abdul-Jabbar of the Milwaukee Bucks. Reed did a great job against both stars and the Knicks advanced to the championship round. This set up a meeting with Wilt Chamberlain and the Los Angeles Lakers. Reed was exhausted at this point. Nevertheless, he kept Chamberlain under control, and the Knicks won two of the first four games.

In Game 5, disaster struck. Reed tore a muscle in his leg and fell to the floor in agony. The Knicks won the game, but they lost their most important player. Without a big man to guard Chamberlain, New York was helpless. The Los Angeles star scored 45 points in Game 6, as the Lakers crushed the Knicks by 22 points.

Game 7 was set for Madison Square Garden. New York fans had little hope that their Knicks would win. The players on both teams seemed to feel this way, too. But right before tip-off, Reed trotted into the arena. The crowd went crazy and Reed's teammates fed off that energy.

Reed could barely move, but he scored the first basket of the game over Chamberlain—who was still amazed that Reed was

WALT FRAZIER

able to play. On defense, Reed used his body to keep the Los Angeles center away from the basket. The rest of the Knicks came to the aid of their leader, especially Walt Frazier. He played one of the best all-around games ever in the NBA Finals with 36 points and 19 assists. The Knicks won the championship, and Reed was named the series Most Valuable Player (MVP).

LEFT: Willis Reed was often asked to sign this photo of him leaving the court after his injury in Game 5.　**ABOVE**: Walt Frazier took control of Game 7 after Reed's fast start.

WAIT . . . WHAT?

The Knicks' first scoring leader was an **All-American** in three sports. Bud Palmer led the team in scoring in 1946–47 using something few basketball fans had seen at the time: a jump shot. Palmer was the kind of athlete who could do just about anything he wanted. In college at Princeton University, he was an All-American in basketball, soccer, and lacrosse—three *very* different sports!

ABOVE: Bud Palmer was a three-sport star in college. He later became a successful sportscaster.   RIGHT: Walt Frazier models one of his dazzling outfits outside a New York hotel.

DID YOU KNOW?

Two Knicks had their basketball skills stolen by aliens. Patrick Ewing and Larry Johnson played themselves in the 1996 movie *Space Jam*. They were two of the five NBA stars whose stolen talents *transformed* the Nerdlucks into the Monstars. Fortunately, Michael Jordan and Bugs Bunny joined forces on the Tune Squad to defeat the Monstars in an exciting basketball game—and return the hoops skills to Ewing and Johnson.

DID YOU KNOW?

Walt Frazier was the best-dressed athlete in New York. He loved to wear stylish suits, overcoats, and wide-brimmed hats. Frazier was nicknamed "Clyde" after the 1930s gangster Clyde Barrow of Bonnie and Clyde. He was often pictured in magazines and newspapers wearing the most fashionable clothes around. Frazier wrote a book entitled *Rockin' Steady: A Guide to Basketball and Cool.*

UNBELIEVABLE!

Every player in the NBA knows he must be ready to step up when his teammates go down. With the Knicks, this is a team tradition. Even so, New York fans prepared for the worst when Carmelo Anthony and Amar'e Stoudemire were injured in February 2012. Everyone knew that it would be difficult to replace their two best scorers.

After several losses, coach Mike D'Antoni looked down to the very end of his bench and decided to give Jeremy Lin a chance. Lin was in his second season and had little experience. In a game against the New Jersey Nets, he scored a career-high 25 points and led the Knicks to a 99–92 win. In the next game, against the Utah Jazz, Lin scored 28 points in a 99–88 victory. He had 23 points and 10 assists in the game after that, as the Knicks beat the Washington Wizards.

Lin's biggest test came in a home game against the Los Angeles Lakers. Superstar Kobe Bryant predicted he would bring the rising star back down to earth. Imagine Kobe's surprise when Lin torched him for 38 points in another victory!

New York City was now gripped by "Lin-sanity." Jeremy was all

Jeremy Lin's amazing run earned him the cover of *SLAM Magazine.*

anyone could talk about. How could a guy that no one had ever heard of suddenly be playing like a Hall of Famer? Not even Lin himself could answer this question.

Three days after beating the Lakers, Lin nailed a 3-pointer at the buzzer against the Toronto Raptors to deliver another thrilling win. That gave him at least 20 points and seven assists in each of his first five NBA starts. No one in league history had done that before.

Lin had another great game against the Dallas Mavericks. The Mavs tried every defense they could think of, but Lin still *racked up* 28 points and 14 assists in a 104–97 win. Lin's amazing run finally ended with a knee injury.

After the season, he left New York to play for the Houston Rockets. Lin appeared in only 26 games for the Knicks, but they were 26 games that no one will ever forget.

IT'S ABOUT TIME

The basketball season is played from October through June. That means each season takes place at the end of one year and the beginning of the next. In this timeline, the accomplishments of the Knicks are shown by season.

1950-51
The Knicks reach the NBA Finals for the first time.

1969-70
The Knicks win their first NBA championship.

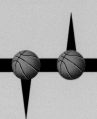 

1946-47
The Knicks play their first BAA season.

1964-65
Willis Reed is the NBA **Rookie** of the Year.

1972-73
New York wins its second championship.

KNICKERBOCKERS vs PHILADELPHIA
NEW YORK CELTICS vs. GLOBETROTTERS
XAVIER vs. ST. ANN'S
MADISON SQUARE GARDEN   JANUARY 1, 1950
26¢ N.Y.C. SALES TAX ¼   25¢

This program shows what a Knickerbocker looked like.

Jerry Lucas helped the Knicks win the 1972–73 NBA title.

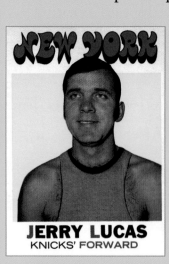

NEW YORK

JERRY LUCAS
KNICKS' FORWARD

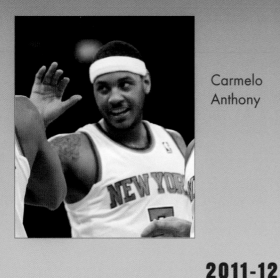

Carmelo
Anthony

Julius
Randle

1984-85
Bernard King leads
the NBA in scoring.

2011-12
Tyson Chandler is
named Defensive
Player of the Year.

2021-22
RJ Barrett becomes the
youngest Knick to average
20 points a game.

1985-86
Patrick Ewing is named
Rookie of the Year.

2012-13
Carmelo Anthony leads
the league in scoring.

2019-20
Julius Randle is
named the NBA
Most Improved Player.

RJ Barrett goes
one-on-one with a
defender. He was
a solid scorer in his
years with the Knicks.

THAT'S A FACT

STREAKY

During the 2022–23 season, Jalen Brunson scored 25 or more points eight games in a row. That broke the team record for guards, set by Dick Barnett in 1965.

FEELING BUBBLY

One of the Knicks' first All-Stars was center Nat Clifton. He was nicknamed "Sweetwater" because of his love for soda pop.

GROUND BREAKER

Willie Naulls was named captain of the Knicks in the 1950s. He was the first African American captain in any of the four major professional sports.

ABOVE: Sweetwater Clifton defends against George Mikan of the Lakers.
RIGHT: Nate Robinson throws one down during the NBA Slam Dunk Contest.

50-50

In 1984, Bernard King scored 50 points against the Spurs. The next night he dropped 50 on the Mavericks. King was the first player in 17 years with back-to-back 50-point games.

RISING TO THE OCCASION

At 5'9" tall, Nate Robinson was one of the shortest players in the NBA. However, his leaping ability was out of this world. He once blocked a shot by Hall of Famer Yao Ming, who stood 7'6". Robinson became a Knicks legend when he won the 2006 NBA Slam Dunk contest. He won again in 2009 and 2010.

RUNNING THE TABLE

In a 1972 game against the Milwaukee Bucks, the Knicks trailed 86–68 in the fourth quarter. They scored 19 straight points to win 87–86. It was the greatest comeback in NBA history.

SPEAKING OF BASKETBALL

"As long as we win, I don't care how many points I score."

► **PATRICK EWING,** *on why he always focused on defense*

"On a particular night, no matter what you do, there's a feeling it's going to work. It's an incredible feeling. There's nothing like it."

► **BERNARD KING,** *on what it is like to get hot in an NBA game*

"When I was there, it was one of the greatest times to be in New York."

► **PHIL JACKSON,** *on the Knicks' championship teams of the 1970s*

"I expect myself to be the best player I can be. I really believe I can be one of the best who's ever played. That's how hard I work."

▶ **JALEN BRUNSON,** *on what it takes to star in the NBA*

"I wanted to be a Knick, I wanted to be one of the greats here."

▶ **JULIUS RANDLE,** *on playing his best in front of the crowds in New York*

"If the ball was up for grabs, I wanted my share."

▶ **HARRY GALLATIN,** *on how he led the NBA in rebounds*

"Go for the moon. If you don't get it, you'll still be heading for a star."

▶ **WILLIS REED,** *on aiming high*

LEFT: Phil Jackson
ABOVE: Harry Gallatin

ROAD TRIP

For fans of the Knicks, all roads lead to New York. But each journey begins somewhere else. Match the pushpins on these maps to the Team Facts, and you will discover the ultimate Knicks road trip!

TEAM FACTS

1. **NEW YORK, NEW YORK**—The Knicks have played here since the 1946–47 season.
2. **PHILADELPHIA, PENNSYLVANIA**—Earl Monroe was born here.
3. **CLEVELAND, OHIO**—Charles Oakley was born here.
4. **LOUISVILLE, KENTUCKY**—Allan Houston was born here.
5. **DETROIT, MICHIGAN**—Dave DeBusschere was born here.
6. **DALLAS, TEXAS**—Willie Naulls was born here.
7. **LOS ANGELES, CALIFORNIA**—Jeremy Lin was born here.
8. **ATLANTA, GEORGIA**—Walt Frazier was born here.
9. **HICO, LOUISIANA**—Willis Reed was born here.
10. **TULSA, OKLAHOMA**—John Starks was born here.
11. **ROME, ITALY**—Andrea Bargnani was born here.
12. **KINGSTON, JAMAICA**—Patrick Ewing was born here.
13. **PORT HARCOURT, NIGERIA**—Precious Achiuwa was born here.

Andrea Bargnani

HONOR ROLL

The great Knicks teams and players have left their marks on the record books. These are the best of the best!

KNICKS ACHIEVEMENTS

ACHIEVEMENT	SEASON	ACHIEVEMENT	SEASON
Eastern Conference Champions	1950–51	Eastern Conference Champions	1971–72
Eastern Conference Champions	1951–52	Eastern Conference Champions	1972–73
Eastern Conference Champions	1952–53	NBA Champions	1972–73
Eastern Conference Champions	1969–70	Eastern Conference Champions	1993–94
NBA Champions	1969–70	Eastern Conference Champions	1998–99

Willis Reed, Patrick Ewing, and Dave DeBusschere rank among the all-time great Knicks.

KNICKS AWARD WINNERS

ROOKIE OF THE YEAR

Willis Reed	1964–65
Patrick Ewing	1985–86
Mark Jackson	1987–88

ALL-STAR GAME MVP

Willis Reed	1969–70
Walt Frazier	1974–75

NBA FINALS MVP

Willis Reed	1969–70
Willis Reed	1972–73

COACH OF THE YEAR

Red Holzman	1969–70
Pat Riley	1992–93
Tom Thibodeau	2020–21

NBA MVP

Willis Reed	1969–70

SLAM DUNK CHAMPION

Kenny Walker	1988–89
Nate Robinson	2005–06
Nate Robinson	2008–09
Nate Robinson	2009–10
Obi Toppin	2021–22

SIXTH MAN AWARD

Anthony Mason	1994–95
John Starks	1996–97
J.R. Smith	2012–13

DEFENSIVE PLAYER OF THE YEAR

Tyson Chandler	2011–12

ABOVE: Anthony Mason
LEFT: Red Holzman

43

NOTHING BUT NET

When a Knick takes aim at the basket, fans hope he hits nothing but net. That is one way of describing a perfect shot in basketball. It does not touch the backboard or the rim and makes a swishing sound that is music to a player's ears. In the NBA, defense is important, but scoring is the name of the game.

The team record for points in a season was set in 1989–90 by Patrick Ewing. He scored 2,347 points and averaged 28.6 per game that year. Ewing's total broke the team record of 2,303 points, set in 1961–62 by Richie Guerin.

In a 2014 game against the Charlotte Bobcats, Carmelo Anthony made 23 of 35 shots and was 10-for-10 from the foul line. He finished the game with 62 points—the most in his career and the most ever by a Knick. His amazing game included a basket made from halfcourt in the final seconds of the first half.

Anthony broke the team record of 60 points, which had belonged to Bernard King. King also held the record for points by a Knick in a playoff game. He scored 46 against the Detroit Pistons in 1984. That team mark lasted until Jalen Brunson scored 47 against the 76ers in Game 4 of their playoff series in 2024. The rest of the Knicks scored a total of 50 points in the 97–92 victory over Philadelphia. Brunson also had 10 assists in the game. Two days earlier, in Game 3, Brunson had 39 points and 13 assists. That made him only the second player in history to create 70 points for his team twice in a row.

Carmelo Anthony could score from anywhere on the court.

GLOSSARY

BASKETBALL WORDS

ALL-AMERICAN—A college athlete recognized as being among the best in the nation.

ALL-STARS—Players recognized as being among the best in the league who are chosen for the annual NBA All-Star Game.

ATLANTIC DIVISION—A grouping of NBA teams that play near the East Coast of the United States.

BALL-HANDLER—A player with dribbling and passing skills.

BASKETBALL ASSOCIATION OF AMERICA (BAA)—A professional league that began play in the 1946–47 season. After three seasons, the BAA joined forces with the older National Basketball League to form the National Basketball Association (NBA).

CONTENDER—A team or player good enough to win a championship.

NATIONAL BASKETBALL ASSOCIATION (NBA)—A professional league that began in 1946 as the Basketball Association of America and changed its name after merging with the National Basketball League in 1949.

NATIONAL BASKETBALL LEAGUE (NBL)—A professional league that began play in 1937–38 and merged with the BAA in 1949–50 to become the NBA.

NBA FINALS—The championship series of professional basketball.

PLAYOFFS—The games played after the regular season that lead to the championship finals.

RELEASED—Let go of the basketball.

ROOKIE—A player in his first professional season.

SWEPT—Finished without losing a game.

VOCABULARY WORDS

ACCURATE—Successful in reaching a target.

AGGRESSIVE—Ready or likely to attack.

ARMORY—A place where military equipment is stored.

BITTER—Angry or hurt because of past experiences.

CHEMISTRY—The blending of talent and personality of two or more people.

COLONIAL—From a time when America was a colony belonging to Great Britain.

DOMINANT—More powerful than anyone else.

ERA—A period of history.

INGREDIENT—Part of a recipe.

LOGO—A design or symbol used by a business.

OFFICIAL—Recognized by the highest authority.

PRESENCE—The impressive appearance of someone.

PROFESSIONAL (PRO)—Done as a paying job.

PROMOTE—Increase recognition and popularity of something.

RACKED UP—Added to a total. The expression comes from the sport of pool.

RUGGED—Tough and determined.

SHOWERED—Given a great amount of something.

STRATEGIES—Plans for success.

TRANSFORMED—Made a big change in something.

UNSELFISH—Willing to share.

URGED—Strongly encouraged.

VERSATILE—Able to do many things.

ABOUT THE AUTHOR

MARK STEWART has written more than 50 books for kids on pro and college basketball. He grew up in New York City rooting for the Knicks and Nets, and played in pick-up games in some of the city's toughest playgrounds. Mark comes from a publishing family. His parents edited and wrote for national magazines and his grandfather was Sunday Editor of *The New York Times*. After graduating with a degree in history from Duke University, Mark wrote for sports and lifestyle magazines and published his first book in 1992. Since then, he has profiled more than 1,000 athletes, many of whom were Knicks—including Carmelo Anthony, Larry Johnson, Jeremy Lin, Stephon Marbury, Connie Simmons, J.R. Smith, and Amar'e Stoudemire. In the 1990s, Mark wrote a children's book with Anthony Mason. As a young fan and later as a sportswriter, Mark met Bill Bradley, Dave DeBusschere, Earl Monroe, and Patrick Ewing. He always wanted to meet Walt Frazier but never did. One night his mother came home from a party and told Mark she had danced with a tall man name Walt who said he played basketball for a living—but forgot to ask for an autograph. He nearly lost his mind.

ON THE ROAD

NEW YORK KNICKS

Two Penn Plaza
New York, NY 10121

NAISMITH BASKETBALL HALL OF FAME

1000 Hall of Fame Avenue
Springfield, Massachusetts 01105

ON THE BOOKSHELF

To learn more about the sport of basketball, look for these books at your library or bookstore:

- Berglund, Bruce. *Basketball GOATs: The Greatest Athletes of All Time.* North Mankato, MN: Capstone Press, 2021.

- Flynn, Brendan. *The Genius Kid's Guide to Pro Basketball.* Mendota Heights, MN: North Star Editions, 2022.

- Peel, Dan. *NBA Legends: Discover Basketball's All-time Greats.* Chicago, IL: Sona Books, 2021.

INDEX

PAGE NUMBERS IN **BOLD** REFER TO ILLUSTRATIONS.